My Dear, Love Hasn't Forgotten You

OTHER BOOKS
BY CAROLYN RIKER

Blue Clouds
This is Love

My Dear,
Love Hasn't Forgotten You

POETRY & PROSE

CAROLYN RIKER

2019
GOLDEN DRAGONFLY PRESS

Dedicated to
Kyle, Genevieve and Copper.
I love you.

CONTENTS

SECTION 3   43
Sensitivity & Seasons

SECTION 4   83
Dreams & Passions

Introduction

I never quite know how to introduce a new set of poems because I've been wearing them, and my heart is exposed. This collection holds me together as much as it frees me. Poetry is an artistic expression of my everything.

Patti Smith, an American singer-songwriter, musician, author, and poet skillfully captured the sensibilities of a poet: *"You write poetry books that maybe 50 people read. And you just keep doing your work because you have to, because it's your calling."*

Later that same day synchronicity bewitched me when I read the words of Dr. James Hollis, a Jungian psychoanalyst and author:

"We may choose careers, but we do not choose vocation. Vocation chooses us. To choose what chooses us is a freedom the by-product of which will be a sense of rightness and a harmony within, even if lived out in a world of conflict, absent validation, and at considerable personal cost."

Hollis continues, *"vocation, even in the most humble of circumstances, is a summons to what is divine... ultimately, our vocation is to become ourselves, in the thousand, thousand variants we are."*[1]

How true. *I have to* write. It is my vocation. My calling. And nearly every day I sit down at the kitchen table, sometimes my desk, or the back porch, and write. I stare out the window and look at the trees. I follow the flight of a hummingbird. I welcome the garden bunnies. My ginger kitty is the best listener. He seems to know when to herd me to a flat surface to close my eyes and give my thoughts a deep rest. I daydream frequently and have notebooks nearby for when words are heard in the liminal shade of spirit, I must write them.

This often brings me tears. Tears and poetry are the closest language to all things divine, unspoken, spoken and felt.

With that, as you read along, please know my spirit is with you in these pages.

Much love,
Carolyn

---

[1] Hollis, James. *Finding Meaning in the Second Half of Life*. New York: Penguin Random House, 2005.

Acknowledgments

I am deeply grateful for the endless support and love of my immediate family and dear friends because without you this book would never have made it here. I'm also deeply grateful for the beautiful work of Alice Maldonado Gallardo, who is the magic behind Golden Dragonfly Press, a small publishing house located in Amherst, Massachusetts.

SECTION 1

❦

Moods & Such

The sky fell silent
and the moon held her hand
when an angel appeared.
Her hair the color of night
and a voice the shade of cobalt;
it summoned a voice
from the deepest blues...

My dear, love hasn't forgotten you.

Let It Be

I didn't mean
to slip through
forlorn borders
but stillness
crafted a key
into the shape of me
and whale blue notes
wept so softly
let it be
let it be
let it be.

What Holds Me Steady

It's been a few days
baptized with rains and hails
that carpeted the ground
with a welcomed early kiss
from winter.

It's been a few days
where my words
have been sifted
through cheesecloth
stretched between mountains
and hummingbirds have stitched
a fine lace along their edges.

It's been a few days
with my prayers up,
head down and heart open
to hear a new way
to river what and when and why.

It's been a few days
of virgin spaciousness
that needs a carefulness
likened to a talisman
as it coaxes a compass of compassion.

It's been a few days
with the shades of saltwater shoals
and jetties of granite's imagination.

It's been a few days
where I've become origami
and shifted into the creases
to celebrate how I'm learning
that slower is what holds me steady.

Loneliness vs. Solitude

Walking beside loneliness
is different
than being immersed
in chosen solitude.

She's that woman
who gathers,
the bruised pears
next to the overripe mangos
with her greying hair twisted above nape.

Solitude is a woolen coat wrapped
next to a complex silk paisley
scarf, as it escapes the skins
of loose garlic cloves,
that freely spill over parsley.

Each gathers the components
for whatever it is that they
will feast. Loneliness compounds
the ripe bruises. Solitude willingly
escapes from the spill
with sublime ease.

Feelings Can Be Our Teachers

It's hard to breathe
the mist of memories
rising soundlessly
across subterranean hills
seeping into the present
not fully welcomed
and yet,
here they are
to be held, watched,
navigated, seen
and respected
so, the past isn't repeated.
Learnt from
riding a bike and feeling
the sensation of flying
down,
down,
down
the steepest of hills
to believe
joy,
love,
hope,
laughter
can also be our teacher.

Dear Self

Don't forget to look at the whole page
and not only that one spot
that hurts
under a blazing sun.

Walk with me
into the shadows
of slower and quieter
letting our eyes close
as a prayer frames a safe cove.

Tell me, once again,
how it'll be okay
as pines grow
and the yellowest finches
gather a bouquet
of feathers for its nest.

Much like hearts mend
and expand and break
and give something
of ourselves as we
nest into the gifting
of our dearest self.

Be Still

Maybe there's nothing *still* about a—*still life.*

Maybe it is a symbol of seasons, a circle, a particle, a nucleus.

Maybe it's our soul's energy that turns stillness into thickets and the winds become our oceans where we wander with quiet's hand reminding us to *'still this life'* while it continuously ripples.

The arrangement of life's objects appears linear, but it isn't—because we aren't.

We are as diverse as spices that flavor this land and our dreams are the connections.

Nevertheless, maybe we need pockets of—*still life*—so we can hear these continuous dream voices—symbols to bring us to our soul's home.

Solitude

When life feels opaque
as if the threads are snared
along a cliff of disbelief
and the music of sunlight
can't discover you,
let solitude welcome you.

Glass Bell

Every snowflake
is a glass bell
pressing my heart
to hear the soul of the earth
and I can't help but to weep
for its beauty
has the profundity
of angels as they speak.

When It Feels Just Right

Sometimes
when all the colors
are rinsed from the sky
but grey remains
it feels just right.

Almost delicious
in a quiet comforting way,
like an omelet and toast and tea
for dinner.

It invites a woolen whisper,
you're doing just right.
Turn down the comforter
and climb in.
Rest tonight.

And tomorrow
I'll bring you
a bouquet
of sunrise.

Sensitivity

I thought of a thousand *wings* to write
but then my attention was drawn
to the sound of nothingness
and the wholeness
of a swallowed horizon
inside an hourglass
washed up along a coast
of sensitivity.

Feelings felt soft and warm
cradled in serenity;
a turtle dove of love's loving
sipped between coffee and
a breakfast cookie
wherein sweetness lies
in autumn's show
of how to let go
when permission is granted
and taught by each leaf
as their prayers lie
face to face
with the hands of the earth
holding this moment of peace.

Home

What if dragonfly's wings
were really stained-glass
painted by the caress
of a hummingbird's tongue?

What if the skies
were an elaborate canvas
of ribbons woven to the hum
of a celestial song?

And we learned
to flow with life's rivers and let
us be drenched with the axil
of earth's ministering; united with the
eclipse of our gifted songs?

What if we surfed the textures,
through forested degrees of our being,
as skyscrapers and people meet us
and as gratefully as trees feed us?

Somehow knowing the *what ifs* are real,
to stretch and complete us.
And our shadows will be as visible
as our quirks reveal us.

What if each day-night,
we find ourselves dancing
with the dreams of
how much life is a script
that hasn't been fully read
and acted upon?

Realizing in flickers
all this seeking
is who
we have already become.

Rhythm & Blues

I suppose
shades of blue
are my go-to.

But then the trees
open to a page of
fawn and I'm
fickle to her hues.

Sun parts through
flat cream clouds
and again, I can't
stop staring,
I know it is rude.

Roses part me
to the left and
grey's sweater
folds me to the right.

How captivating
to be orchid rare
and render the
soul's sound in
her yellow's might.

Quiet is the color
of midnight, juxtaposing
with the silence of an
unfolding spring's mood.

Sadness cultivates
an arpeggio returning
to the deepest colors
expressed as
Rhythm and Blues.

A Soul's Print

And then the sun
silenced the moon's thoughts
as if she wasn't there,
but she was.

Always feeling what isn't noticed;
the roots of being bypassed
and discounted as her shadow flared.

She threw a lasso over summer
and rested in the grasses,
realizing betrayal wouldn't hurt as much,
if she didn't care.

But she does
and always will.
Finding answers in the shadows
where beauty isn't a myth;
it's a soul print we all deeply share.

Ocean

Sometimes
when the colors
of everything collide
and those vibrations crave
the wisdom of the sea,
one must stop
and center into
an ethereal zero of holy.

Ocean blue
meets a cosmic destiny
and the salt of the earth
can taste the shores of silent,
transparent as air,
the heartbeat of water
inside the fluidity founded
in the home of soul's eyes
where inner truth is aware.

Allow Yourself to Be Very Still

*Y*ou can't push what isn't ready to grow. You can't dream until you let go.

You can though, let those pregnant ideas germinate with the darkest nights and richest mulch and fairest depth of the seas.

Where sturgeons swim through arches of your imagination while you rest and rest and dream those hidden parts of you.

And the cycles of rinse and dry repeat are the portals of your mind's eye that truly sees.

You allow yourself to be very still so that a feather will lead you along a pond of gold and birds become your singing.

That trill of knowing, you are without a doubt, a spiritual creature living in a world that can barely see how the in between spaces are the treasures of detaching under and through to the spirit world where dreams surface back to here and translate as poetry.

SECTION 2

✿

Creativity & Love

"I just called to say I love you
I just called to say how much I care, I do
I just called to say I love you
And I mean it from the bottom of my heart."

— STEVIE WONDER

A Creative's Creed

It takes a poet to squeeze love from a lemon and to feel its sunshine.

It takes an artist to paint their soul for all to see but few to believe.

It takes a musician to find the somber notes to sing the deepest, roundest Blues.

It takes a writer many lifetimes to story a book.

It takes a lover to show how vulnerable can speak the tender inside of real truths.

It takes grief to show the holiness in sadness.

It takes all of us to share our ordinary and extraordinary gifts to mix and mix until there's a swath of canvas peppered with uniqueness—where we dance and dance to the curve of a raindrop, pinned to a sky, spinning on a rocky orb—together.

You and I are the "us."

Let's hold this kismet which paints our souls, so we can sing the deepest felt Blues, and share our vulnerable with a sacred few, and respect each other in joys and holy sadness too.

Where life cycles through me and touches you.

Together we can foster the essence of humanity, a bridge which is poetic in its diversity—a song that clearly sings of truth.

Childlike Soul

What if we gave the child,
a bucket of ribbons,
papier-mâché and paints
with no rules
except
be messy and create?

What if
what divides us
from the child inside us
is the real key
to help us to see?

Maybe she is showing us
the way that strays us and
turns us into sharp pointy fractions
with sad shoulders and swollen toes
that blind our ability to play.

Can we for just a tiny moment
forget about the pains
that trickle in like rains
cementing those stains
on our heart's flow?

Let's practice together
and stroll with a little simple,
holding hands with stardust
letting silly swing us
as treetops laugh with us
welcoming us back
inside our heart's
childlike prose.

Picasso's Fireflies

Pen me lyrics
straight from your heart.
Release the filters
of unsure.
Let the word's spirit
explore.

Tell me your dreams,
your thoughts,
hopes and wishes.

Let's paint them,
sing them,
dance them,
play them
on a hard night's sky
where starlight resembles
Picasso's fireflies.

Breathe with me
inside a sun's river
that puddles
on the earth.

Let's walk with
the footsteps of fern
and evergreen
and feel
the heartbeat of sound
and the energy that's seen.

Bless us gentle
as prayer hands form
on the tips of trees.
This love holds holy
in the landscape
of humanity.

The Profundity of Being

At the end of the day
when sound grows dim
and questions remain...

Who is there for you
when you are not strong
enough to carry the moon?
And how will the stars
pin to a bleak sky?

At the end of the day
when the grasses are still
and rose shelters with thorn,
who will you tell...?

That your heart is bruised
the color of earth
and that green
is drained to grey.

At the end of the day
where will you go
when you gave
and what you did
has been weighted
against you?

This is a crack. A fall. A heavy prayer.
A profundity of being
so damn human
it aches.

You are being unearthed.

Questions shine their brightest in darkness.
And those answers bring you closer to your soul's worth.

What Poetry Means to Me

*P*oetry needs space to have her roots spread like a million fibers connecting the present to a river of divinity.

Poetry is the spaciousness of valleys and the footsteps turned to mountains as well as the safety of a harbor where darkness is lit by the phases of the moon within.

Poetry is a destiny that can taste the lips of a leaf and breathes the colors of mercury.

Poetry is a dream birthed from one's soul brought to life with each letter touching her notes of transparency.

Poetry is raw, real, and pure; it is the spirit under the chaos and the very real dragons battled within. The demons and angels and the voices are often heard and necessary to field the conflicts of understanding, the dance of relationships, the revolving translucent doors leading to infinity; the prose is endless.

Poetry is an undulating release, an explanation of the untold, and the truest identity given from the source of one's soul.

The Giving of You

I'm going to give you a handful of wildflowers
so, each petal that falls will remind you
that the earth breathes, and the moon rises.

Sorrow is not only reserved for death
but for not living our deepest soul truths.

Fetter not the ways of the past but give the giving of you.
Challenges are cardinal cups of courage
supported by the eyes of the heart,
the solution of solitude,
the sit-with-me-quiet.

The wants are real.
The questions that layer over flatlands
bend with the scent of rain
before its birth reaches you.

There will always be a cluster of promises
that will break us
and then sees us
for what is our truest true.

This is How I Write

W riting is more than words. For me, what creates love in a sentence is the rhythm. The shorter sentences unite with longer ones and each creates a breath; it's a literary variation of a ménage à trois that my heart can fully accept because it's the bud embracing the bloom and the entirety of Nature supporting me.

Writing is the sequence where vulnerable can be felt and spoken as lovingly as music moves one's heart through a salsa merging at the rivers of one's soul.

Poignantly, powerfully, parched emotions playfully pirouette into the thickets of lush.

>The greens of a mossy bed.
>The quiet heat of blue flame.
>Anger without the thunder of accusations.
>Fear and shame surrender in tender.
>The anguish of moving over edges
>and the freefall of fluidity's flight.

This is how I write.

Bearing my heart in rivulets to traverse the gorge of unseen to express my soul's tongue. It cries me tendrils of real founded in the freedom of this earned island of solitude; not lonely but with words as my deepest companion.

The Artist Knows

*A*n artist will tease out the bones of a feeling and re-store the fragments with ink from their soul. In such a way they use a palette of sensual to expose and move with an unforeseen spell.

It's magic and it isn't.
It is painful and it isn't.
It is exhausting and it isn't.

There's little escape but there is.

The worn steel wool barnacles, of an artist's vessel, will sum-mon the invisible into the tangible.

As much as anger is guava nectar on fire.
Sadness becomes mired lily pads.
Fear tastes the inside of a turtle's shell.
Joy that dances us free is music that sees us.

Love protects and bends and holds the cosmos to propagate creativity so that imagination can suspend stories long enough to enter through unseen doors and visit so the truths can be held, told, and supported.

A Slow Dance

*T*iming, pacing ourselves, finding we have seeds in our heart's pockets just waiting, wanting and needing to grow however sometimes we need sacred space to connect heart, mind, and soul.

Those three dances are a slow dance of infinity.

Poetic at times, contemplative, happy, darker, deeper, with sentient trees as our soul's speaker. We wait with our hand to our heart pressing gently but firmly into the center.

Under all the chaos and doubts we spiral a beautiful modern expressive dance. The spotlight holds and focuses a sensitive blend of emotions through the voices reaching the shoulders, swaying an eclipse with hips, body flowing as a gentle rain lets the mind connect with the heart—a sensuous pulse is the dance.

Love and the Fruit Tree

Love is like a fruit tree.
In winter
she's the silent sound
of leafless
but her inner circles ring.

I hear her barren branches
bear wild blooms
and ghost bees bring nectar
to turn her fruit.

The seasons unfold her bold.
Love grows her heavier
and branches bend –
it gives and takes us
through storm it warms.

Love bears us fruit
on the shy nigh
of our highest form.
The gnarled branches transcend
what is and isn't.

Love's core carries her seeds.
It's well planted
in the palms of her hands
and welcomes
the ranges of grief and joy
to water her land.

There – I don't know exactly where
but I feel love
becomes the sun and moon;
the sweetness born
of barren branches –
aged from her wildest blooms.

Show and Feel

Show, don't tell,
has been said to writers.
I say, show and feel
the wrinkles of grey
outlining the quiver
of silence's rise and
opal dreams sprinkled
with braver cries.

Those that only show
can sketch
from a river of sky
where thought streams
may collide.

Maybe it's impossible
for poets to hide
the abundance of moons inside
when their heart is carved
from the clouds of a sunrise.

A Love Story

*Y*ou say, *be strong and how you believe me* but as you speak, I feel the falling sun and starless skies become a sadness that has shared my destiny.

You say, *it's all good* but you forget those words trace the hole inside that grows a garden of my circled moonless midnights.

You say, *take care* and yet you overlook how you have a love although it's not my time.

You say, *you're sorry* and with this—we finally agree.

My soulmate has yet to be who shares my dreams, and when it happens, we will stroll along wide sands and exchange loneliness with a love that understands.

I'll say to you, *thank you for believing in me when I wasn't strong. Those doubts became me, and midnights were my garden song.*

You'll smile and say, *I've often asked the spirits for someone to see what I see in you.*

And then a silence that only real can have when hearts agree:

I never meant to hurt you. I could only love you as a friend and not the soulmate I dreamt we could be.

Journey

*A*long our intimate rivers of awareness we are cradled by reflections, and insights as we begin to acknowledge how the phases we are in are parallel to our inner and outer resources; be it parched, stuck, frozen, quiet, joyed, supported, blurred—this nebulous may feel like chaos but it is precisely where we learn to see patches of ebony and gold guiding us in our journey.

These incantations are a sweet, sweet holding that leads to surrendering, giving, and affirming our boundaries and expressing how our creativity understands as all our parts are a whole.

When Love Is Real

I could pen
something light
but there
my love wouldn't be real.

Like when the sun
becomes wind,
it holies my feels.

Like a flute
carved from a
hidden beam
inside of a
rapturous dream.

When love isn't real,
it can hope too much
under a wrong tree,
next to a windmill
that exposes my fate
and becomes sad notes.

And the Blues play me
as much as my mistakes
knowing this love
is not an escape.

There's a quality inside
such a holy sun-wind
that gently speaks
a truer tree
will plant next to you.

This love you seek
will know you
because the branches
speak a similar truth.

Inside of You

Only you can follow
how the sun goes down
along the breastbone
of your shadow.

Only you can blend
with the pulse of a bird
sensing their silent
downy brown.

Only you can wait
for the moon to return
as a balloon lowering
its string of truth.

Only you can summon
orcas and dolphins
while listening to
a breeze of Maple leaves.

Only you can see
the color of sound
when it emerges
from darkness to dawn.

Only you can honor
your boundaries
when the tides turn inward
and the blessings of less is more.

Only you can love
from what is shown
and grown by letting Nature
be your heart's teacher.

Only you can follow and blend
while you wait and heed your call
to see how to honor the spirits
that know you are made of love.

Stop Trying So Hard

I misplaced my glasses
by the blue flowerpot
or maybe not;
perhaps under my chair.

I finally stopped
trying so hard to see
and just listen
to the hyssops
tugging me away
along a full budded tree.

I held on dearly to
to a clover breeze
and saddled up with
a dragon; its allure
incandescently
flung a spell o'er me.

'Till fern's foliage
signaled my venture complete
was I able to see my needs;
a diving quest,
to live the edges fully.

You Are Loved

Greens graciousness
witnessed the stones
where prairies parted,
lavender as the seas
of tiny humming leaves,
that clearly rang
on naked branches
and gathered me
a sacred welcome.

Next to a single tree
who reminded me
how the earth too is invisible,
yet incumbent of its sorcery
as tender roots recited hidden lyrics
parsed along a warm spring's breeze...

You are love.
You are loved.
You are loving.

Relationship

I sat by a familiar stream
that reminded me
when too often I forget
that what was
isn't
and now
the pages are
a soft dove blue
where I can turn and rewrite
how my soul begs
please, sing you true
those ripples that
gather deep over smooth
are spirit and love
it wants me to see
and calls me by name
in a relationship
with self
holding reverence
with solitude.

Pink Rose Slippers

Way out there
where the patches of sun
touch only the water's tips,
there will be a sound
so simple and so equal
as when waves taste
the soul of the earth.

It sings to me greens
like how trees know
the flight of a
fair, fair swallow.

Its soul wears
pink roses as slippers
that have sailed mighty rivers
so blue,
they turn fresh water
into a salty sea.

Without a doubt,
each detail is embroidered
with a lavender sky and
framed in bamboo
while evergreens cast
a sanctity with
long dappled robes
wrapped around
the cries of the
weary.

Rain Dance

I turned up the rain
and together
we danced
to her music.

Grateful for Stillness

It's almost always when
night falls
into the desert
of our soul's rhythm
that we can hear again.

We can hear frost wed grass and
sense how maple combs through
the life circles of a tree.
It makes us weep.

We are more in touch
with the signature
of cotton sheets breathing
with our heart's beat.

Grateful for the stillness
hushed by the stars,
and the scratched penciled thoughts
freed on canary's featherless paper.

This is night.
It wakes us to the home
inside our call.

The Braille Becomes Me

It's raining braille.
I know
because I feel the letters rise
inside
as they meet with my fingertips.

Circling with my unknown's knowing.
Sitting with me.
Passing through a dance of fluidity.

Teaching me the treble and clef
of a deeper melody;
a song that rides
on the streams of infinity.

The circles of our whole.
The sound of zero hums
and its braille becomes me.

SECTION 3

✿

Sensitivity & Seasons

"Clouds come floating into my life,
no longer to carry rain or usher storm,
but to add color to my sunset sky."

—Rabindranath Tagore, *Stray Birds*

Wing and Warble

There's a small space
beneath an owl's wing
and the chin of a hummingbird;
there you can rest.

There's a holy warble
at the crest of a wave
just before it breaks;
there it's safe.

There's a still swallow
exposed on silver leaf.
where a breeze speaks.

There's tragic turmoil
when the innocent
are not seen;
but we must weep.

Chances are...
wing and warble
will wave over us
until we feel safe
and swallows will perch
on silver leaf
to awaken us
and we'll hear
the innocent voices
gathered on a breeze
to comfort gentle souls
lest we forgot and yes,
we will let those tears weep
into a small space,
a sanctuary nested in love.

When the Veil Is Thin

You'll often find me
in the subtle nature
of unseen magic
where the source
of sorcery pivots.

I can't say it only
stays for one eve;
but at the moment
ghost-spirits
are extra close.

That flicker that finds
the waft of chill and
decided wonder,
reassures a mystical
knowledge beyond my soul.

And promises the reflections,
brushing twilight's flannel edges,
like oceans and love and music...

Whispering...
We are truly never alone.

Evolution

A trio of birds
lined a burnt red fence;
a woodpecker's speckles were
dovetailed by two round robins.

I speculated at their wise calling.
It felt almost a warning
with the clouds grey storming and
the ground crawled with a
scuttle of sparrows pawing.

Edges of me peeled up
from my perch
as if I had feathers
and I believe I did,
because the wind began
to lift me
up, up, up
and over an envelope
once sealed
with a deliberate silence
of melted wax
shamed by my changing initials;
not once but thrice.

I needed those birds
to accentuate how it is time
to be the woman whose flight
is less hesitant to speak
when indelible truths are
burnt before her soul's seeing eyes.

How an extension of self
isn't remedied by a union
with another
but the convoluted
evolution when one begins
to trust and believe
in herself.

Writing Solitude

You, a mirage,
roll me
like the pills of wool
scattered on my favorite sweater;
those very sleeves
worn from resting
on a heavy table.

Vacancy sits before me
while the sound of morning's lips
touches the earth
and midnight's dreams
saturate toasty thoughts.

Heart is slathered in the cinnamon
and birds await the breadcrumbs.
Soul searches through the senses
and centers in silence,
where the sigh of solitude isn't lonely
but purposed to be the scaffolding
for sentences to write me
their stories' thoughts.

Be You

Our diversity is a gift.
Our sensitivity is too.
We all have something to share.
Please be you.

My Morning's Quiet

*T*here are moments we are destined to be extra, extra quiet and embodied with the softest pillows that create a barrier away from the harshness of this world.

Where we can simply worship books, fill journals, art, hear paper play with pens and pencils so ideas can freely sprout from the heights of our imagination.

There are moments we may lament with our story still waiting to be birthed. Or to just stay with the still waters of music that hears us so we can temporarily let go of the abundance that demands our attention.

Somehow, when we give our self this sort of permission to slip below the crossfire of perfection, we begin to breathe the air of cobblestones where images are sundry languages and the assortment of accents and letters can calm.

Quiet congregates as a mountainous cathedral, a seaworthy synagogue or a tundra of temples where we learn to follow what calls us, seeks us, speaks us, natures us, comforts us, restores us away from a world that tries to conform us.

Quiet is essential; it is my soul's manifesto.

Now and Tomorrow

Make me one
with the sound of grey clouds
that arch over a sea
and returns me
to the simplicity of awe
connecting my feet
to the grace of land
touching her waters.

All before
the voices were birthed
and the spirits
no longer scattered
as a dandelion's seeded head
goes wild.

Count with me the evergreens
spared by autumn's bare cloak
and let's dream with
our now and tomorrows.

Let's let the old voices
fade from memory's doormat,
next to those skeleton keys
and tuck them warm
with a fresh knitted pattern;
an envelope of tranquility
dipped in a sea with less storms.

I Hear You

*W*atch who is there for you even when the birds have gone silent under a starless night.

Watch who grows quiet with you and lets sentiments shimmer, silent as morning dew; neither for nor against but most importantly—with you.

Watch who supports you when your best isn't, and your faded dreams need a lift and self-doubts collect in the wells of quintessential aloneness.

Watch those who say, *it's nothing* and add a predictable cliché.

Stay closer to those who say, *I hear you.*

And in that tiny crevice of hope, let go of the crowded decay and know it only takes one voice to hear the depth of a swallow's sung sorrow under a starless night held by the moon.

Wed to a Rose

You,
being the fault lines
that show stress fractures
into canyons of folds
robed in blues
wed to a rose
perceived by Nature;
you,
free you
only when
you are you.

Sleepy Clover

The sun spun
a single thread
of solitude
over a fawn stained hill.

Sweeping the grasses
with a finely tuned
ocean of still.

Between the hedges
and sleepy clover,
regrets paused and
clarity candled
contemplation.

The invisible
was purely seen
and what was heard
were angel bells
on the very tips
of an evergreen.

All else ceased to be
as the sun spun
her simplicity.

Waves Kiss the Shore

*R*ide with me to the hillsides where the land brushes our soul with the sea and the scent of solitude are waves kissing the span of the shore.

I'll be smiling as the seasons reach her harbor and the inlets shimmer with the birth of sky's starry seeds.

Knowing the darkness is our light—in you, I see me.

Fully Loved

Can you tell me
the last time
you sang to a rose
and tasted the blush
of her lips
and the scent of her lush?

Can you tell me
the last time
you followed the spirit
of what triggers you
and sipped the succulent wisdom
of what you needed to know?

Can you tell me
the last time you
parted the clouds
with your fingertips
and circled that very
holy place which understands
and expands what really
matters to you?

Can you tell me
the last time you
were fully loved
for your quirks,
all vulnerable and true,
as well as the polished
river rocks that
only see you?

For me...
I'm still learning
to slow down,
just enough,
to unravel
these intimate
mysteries.

Autumn Mood

Of all the seasons
autumn
is my favorite
mood.

My Favorite Color Is Rain

My favorite color is rain.
Especially when
its sounds
gather along
the skirts of dusk.
Where feels can be felt
but thoughts are not.
And the surface of everything
smooths from whence
there was creation.
Perceived by
the breath of swallows
wrapped under the eaves
of home's heavenly hallows.

Blossoms

This is not an ordinary moon.
This one makes me weep
pastel cherry blossoms
on a spring's
nightfall.

An Invisible Orchestra

The sun's sharp edges
were not softened
by leaves
or feathers
but blinded by settling cold.
Winter wrapped grief
over bud free branch;
whereas stillness rocked
with abundance
the pinging chant
of a nuthatch and
her black cap
invited invisible orchestra strings
as we slow danced in the shadows
of sun's setting soul.

The Signature of Our River

Something happens
when we let the clock's tick fade
and the list of to-dos fall
pushing aside the whys and why nots
and only listening
to our soul's sweet call
outside the wild of it all.

And we become the shivers
on winter's sleeve
her branches,
the verily deep
are the bones inside our seeing;
and we find just what we
are looking for.

A signature written on ebony,
followed by ivory,
the taste is complete.
The essence of
every single nuance
sets alive the tapping of our feet;
its rhythm is our river
that we must always seek.

The Sky Showed Me

It was as if
the horizon had bit
into a blood orange
and the juices kissed
the remaining autumn's descent
as winter's signature
began her rising
into a sleepy,
dreaming consent.

Scarlet Dreams

Autumn,
how your skirt
once full
now gifts rubies
to a fading garden.

You teach us stillness,
where enchantment sources
our visions;
such as those
tiny leaves letting go.

l am your quietness,
as my eyes need to close
and wander
with scarlet dreams
and deeper blues.

Where we gather
with souls long ago
and listen
to this season's decay
and invite her living truths.

Nature Completes Me

One of the most
comforting feels
about nature
is it doesn't compete;
it completes us.

The Welcoming

The heavy flow
of a silent snow
made quiet–loud
as tree souls bowed
in a frozen dream
slumbering softly,
whispering prayers
that only spirits hear;
beneath
a fine, fine
snow of welcoming.

Symmetry

I keep thinking
how trees forever meditate
as starlight cares and
Nature explains eternal,
inside the mantra of bees canvassing
the nectar of listening.

I keep believing
how overlapping
the concave of understanding
begins and ends in circles.
Where touch or speech can fill
or break or oppress. The latter
a deforestation of soul.

I keep learning
it's harsh and unnatural
to suppress symmetry
because growth is empirical;
dished from ladles of life's
strict and gentle.

I keep sensing
we are the concourse
of our deepest being;
rinsing with sun and moon
on rapids of sea
casting dreams;
all our cycles are essential.

Witness

Just make sure
there's a patch of color
next to the blue bells
so, she can tend
to the flowers out back.

It is simple like that
to check-in
on those who hold quiet.
Wind and thoughts are similar;
they are endless.

But she died lonely
because few took the time to say,

Are you okay? How are you today?

Except for the wild sweet grasses.
They became her only witness
and so, she gave them
her last smile and breath
because no one else saw
her fade away.

Piano

*J*ust now the sky squeezed the purest sound of silence while pouring a simple glass of water. It amplified an undercurrent of mystery only seen when the air crawls to the wings of alabaster pinks. Inviting me to walk through cherry blossom clouds and over a bridge into the horizon. It was rather refreshing as my finger grazed the cool waters eloping with an invitation to ignore the dryer's beeping and letting practical dissipate to a gentle lullaby captured by piano's keys playing inside of silence's melody.

A Secret Perfume

Such is a petal
who flowers her wick
the width of intelligence
fragile not in character
but appearance renders
her invisible
so much so
that overlooked
is what it is
until she stops
and lays with the earth
to wonder
what secret perfume
emits the courage
it takes to bloom
and bloom.

Fields Grow Poetry

Flowers
paint my bones
with sentimental ink.
Flushing forward
in fields of poetry
to center my soul;
its voice
is my complete.

The Language That Weeps

Two ravens cried
with the voice
of a stormy sky;
it shook me real
and cradled
the opening of my eyes
where compassion
sheltered the essence
with wings;
time turned to flight
where life could speak
the colors of Nature;
it's the language that weeps
the grave sound of
dying clouds
from those whose stories
were never heard
but now their tears
are the source of
our seas.

Those Lazy Bees

When flowers bloom
and reeds brush through
as if to say,
savory sweetly
the seers of early summer.

With slower thoughts
on amber beams,
gives chase to lazy bees
who dance their song
on buds once a dream
now to hear
their tender prose
while shy winds embrace
their fair petaled lace.

Peace

Late summer
left sun puddles,
signing the language of love
with a scent of quiet
so innocent it felt shy
but the wind knew
to ask the earth
for reassurance;
Is this real?
Or is this how
soft feels when
waters nest me
a riverbed
and peace
believes in still.

The Earth Offered Me a Shoulder

I heard the grasses weep
and the clouds heard them too
so, they sent the rains to
softly soothe.

The earth
offered a shoulder
just in case
there was a need to tremble
as grass blades sometimes do.

All I could do
was write for them
a small puddled poem
to ease the reflection
shared with the grasses
and my tears too.

Shaman

There's a cave in my holy,
a thousand birds rest there.

Hummingbirds and sparrows.
Ravens and hawks.
Owls and finches.

The noise is an uproar;
a feathery fusion of flurry.
Sometimes they fly me
along the coast of heart's home;
this is ocean speak.

Or we soar mountains
'til the earth crunches cold
and breathes me deep as if
stardust was oxygen
and mountains are my feet.

I dwell within the bells
of ancient rocks and hear
my firm focus stretch
to the symbolic center where
seers chant
shaman ways and
healers are humble;
they wash my fears
from the tears within the flight
of a thousand years;
it is the singing sound
of my soul's questing.

Soul Basin Song

If you will,
close your eyes
and you might just feel
a fine layer of silt
that has settled
into the soul basin of your song;
where a wave's curl is clear
and the hum of seaweed
is that of a seer.
Just listen.
Answers are near
when the soul of your song
is witnessed.

Footsteps

I could speak
but the hush of twilight
is filled with fawn colors
fading as if footsteps
along a quiet beach
and this leads my eyes to sleep
with dreams of painted tomorrows.

You Are Beautiful

My eyes feel like a camera
but then switch to a waterfall
because the light
touches a tree's leaves
just so,
as if to say,
and maybe it did,
you are beautiful.

Just a Moment

While this envelope
of sentimentality covers me,
there's an innocence
in hearing the wings
of a hummingbird's
splash of redness
converge with the applause
of a fair blueness;
such is the sky
whose backdrop
echoes the answers
flowing inside of
a rose's vibration
and bloom.

Laughter Is Natural

I don't know if I should write this
because what if I pop the moment
with doubt?
And let the sounds of
happiness
skip away
because it is the wrong way.
And yet
this specialness
is pure and priceless;
circles of innocent
jump
up and down
with a round red ball bouncing
in a courtyard
laughing free
and natural
as life could be.

Home

You are home
when love
turns down
the comforter
of your soul.

SECTION 4

✣

Dreams & Passions

"I tore myself away from the safe comfort of certainties
through my love for truth—and truth rewarded me."

— SIMONE DE BEAUVOIR

A Poem Is a Dream

A poem is a dream
and a beginning space
where one part is here
and the other
I'm not sure where she goes
but it happens as easily
as a nuthatch rests freely.

The listening winds answer in
bits and pieces in a familiar
let's go and see
where the threads are bare
and the stitches feel uneven,
pulled out and too shy to tell.

Let's go and see
where we can re-stitch
the lost patches
of that bruised soul
you so often confuse
with wrong
but when
a poem is really a dream
I positively believe
you are the fabric of its song.

Chaos Teaches Us

If we listen carefully
to what's inside of chaos
it might turn into a piece of word fabric
embroidered with our truest emotions.

Like the sound of hibiscus tea
pouring over a mélange of cozy;
it whispers on repeat, *go gently...*
and tucks us under a handstitched quilt
that gives a slight nod of reassurance.

As much as the daffodils do
settled on a wide windowsill;
blue vase holding their prose-like spill,
coaxing our ancient eyes to close,
tired from folding a thousand feels.

If we listen carefully,
as night grows her garden of
sleeps and dreams,
we might just hear Bob Marley sing,
'everything is gonna be alright'
inside the magic of our dreams.

What Is a Soul?

*W*hat is a soul? Has anyone seen one?
What if that rabbit over there with the fair pink petal ears is a soul's voice of nature?

What if laughter, that squeezes tears, is the soul of happiness?

Have you ever felt in awe at the way the sun sets and kisses a fence and paints the shadow of a hummingbird into a masterpiece with its rapid soft winged blinks?

Is this the soul of gratitude?

What about a child who holds your hand and looks up for no reason and smiles?

Is that the soul of trust?

Does a soul have a purpose?

Is it an absolute destiny that evolves before birth as well as death with an inhale and exhale, or a cry with closed eyes?

Can a soul drift to a sea's bed to rest?

Can a soul climb a mountain and stitch a map with pieces of calico handed down from generations to continue the threads expressed in our stories?

Maybe souls are before us and in us and around us; that invisible connection that draws and repels us to each other.

Maybe it's a blank page that's full and yet clear but is revealed when we dip our pen over tender to find our soul is an ink's well seeing us.

An Epic Love Note

It is the rose that speaks
the sea and sky and branches
from her heirloom wisdom
never to abandon but as a eulogy;
it repeats for the living
whose dying is blindly quenched
by false pretense of white man's undoing.

A rose reminds us of her realities,
'we are our ancestor's revolution.
Only together will democracy be.'

And as the day passes
the petals of her skirt fall and decay
to balance the earth's Native truths;
spirits nudge us to know
the bounty of humanity's needs.

A cry to see the epic love notes
served to us by lesser means,
hidden in plain sight such as
the homeless seeded along
their daylight-shadowy plight.

The marginalize who carry
such a deadly weight;
sing from sunlit soul Blues,
till fingers bleed
and we hear the depth of their true; and
the musical riffs are how tree rings first grew.

Diversity brushes the score with ivory and ebony;
the pulse rises and falls with a rhythm of courage.
Vulnerability crests over infinite illusions
and the scales of transparency let us be

the *Muddy Waters* that feeds
our deep-rooted equality
stretched from voices
rising from a rose
to a sea with an unbinding
call for unity.

We Are the Wish

For right now,
let's talk softly
to each other
and we'll become
a love song.

Let's watch the snow
form tiny poems
of crystal fairies
and dance a slow dance
of safe and warm.

For right now,
let's pour cream over oatmeal
and berries and cinnamon too
and let the love infuse
our purpose,
our fullness,
our obligations;
as gentle winged creatures
supplanted from the norm—
for just a few.

Let's hold this vision
of hearing each other
for who and where
and what we are.

And see and be
with us now
not yesteryear
on sorrow's clouds
but as a crystal entity;
freely floating
as if we were
a wish come true
inside a falling star.

Aging Is Just Fine

If you see me
staring at you
it's because
I'm not sure
who you are.

Those aged lines
grow grey wilder
obscure and shapeless
engulfs ample shores.

Eyes-closed-wide
holds shame inside
dismissing swiftly
the how-to-see
with kinder eyes.

What say you
if we smashed the
scale of lies.
Shoved aside those
mind-word knives?

Maybe then,
minus the world's screen,
the depth inside
can be seen.

Bigger Isn't Better

There's a corner of less crowded like the wingspan between shoulder blades hidden in the chambers of our heart's deepest dreams.

A divot of mercy. A basin of compassion, when we hear another's voice crack under the pressures of growing old; the raspy breath not speaking loudly but heard in the silence of how did I get here without living?

What dreams do we smoother for the sake of bigger and better but forgetting the wealth of our soul?

The discovery of our true self is there, when we set aside the demands and expectations of others.

This is not selfish, foolhardy or thoughtless.

It is the meaning of why we are here. To create and declare a deeper psychological interdependence that symbolizes a mutual respect of love, equality, and growth.

Letting our first and last breath be the beginning and the seeds of our tomorrows, exhaled through the giving from our deepest soul.

Becoming

We became aged fruit
and stayed there
until we turned to wine.

Our Wrinkles Know

I want to
sleep next to you
in that curled fashion
of a comma
or in quotations
that repeat
I love you
in whispers
the weight of
fine cotton
and wrinkles are
our known secrets
because age has reached
a stage where words
are in our eyes and
from our hearts.

Welcome to My Daydream

I 'll watch the birds while the kettle heats and daydream. Imaginary you will say something sweet, *Let's go here and there. Let's build a castle. Let's plan. Let's travel. Let's play.*

And I'll reply with a soft alibi, *not today my dear. My heart is on repeat with a personal love story. I need to write. My soul is a poem and desires to restore with quiet's quiet.*

Imaginary you will smile because we both understand that relationships can be apart and together, spacious and close, integrated and independent—we can soak in our similarities and honor the space of our differences; it's a love that welcomes our creativity.

And the kettle will summon me from my reverie. Just like the birds will carry on with feathered ease. And I'll return to the companion of my words.

Just Let Go

I wasn't going to write a poem
but the evergreens said otherwise
on this misty morning
where grey highlights all the feels;
it turns me gypsy-like dancing in the wild.

My breath
becomes the hum of branches
and the eternal paint strokes of layered skies;
seen not but felt with dizzy ease.

Seasons lay
in the stillness of nothingness
repeating circles of music
for us to feed.

Maybe that's why
whales sing a spiral song
in the deepest depths
of my soul's seas.

And here I am
amongst the evergreens,
connected to the earth,
and lifted to the heavens
swimming with
evergreen-whales
just because
I let go
and let it be.

Hush

There's a field of clouds
curved over lily
hushed on bent knee
praying as smooth as slate
to purely be with our dreams
to explore the treasures
of our real
which sparks the soul
to share our passions
and so, we heal.

A Rose Garden

Sensate with me
for a spell
under those grey umbrella clouds
and let's follow the lineage
of our spirit's longing.

Such as roses
left behind
on naked bruised vine
as if the scent of winter's still
completely renders me
and fulfills
something quiet
inside my soul's spiral climb.

I often need
the respite of absurdity
and the fond notes
of ebony caressing ivory;
creativity frees the static of ordinary
and writes the seeds planted before me –
time is a reverie.

Will you please
pause with me
to press into what seems imaginary
but nonetheless the essential elements
of where we are resilient
as we are pliable?

Compare me not,
respect me whole,
see the worthy stains
lingering on my leaf's soul.

And I will say to you,
as if a waterlily prose,
accept my faults
and I will yours.
This is the sunrise
of our beautiful.

My Circles

l gathered grey clouds
from my pockets
and pinned them
to the window
of the sky's soul.

Together we talked
about this and that
and it became very real
how listening matters
and hearing infinity
softens the edges
of my circles.

This is where l don't
quite believe me,
until l close my eyes
and become a dream
dancing with the sky
and my soul.

When Voices Speak

Inside of the first blinks of morning, when quiet is hardly awake, and purpose has been scrubbed softly from memory, there's a smooth surface where dreams perpetuate and hang-glide parallel with the horizon.

You could almost be a ledge and the sun's rising would thank you before hoisting up her sails.

Stay there and breathe with her sweet spirit.

This is the very place where our soul's voices can speak with the rings of the earth; this is the golden knowing of the unknowing.

The keys presented are from inside our past, alchemized through living, translated by our mistakes and released from expectations.

We are given an undefinable fusion that understands less is more.

This refinement of our gifts is so pure, it's endless. It is where our heart blooms and she'll know—this, this is the way.

The Answers Will Come

There's an invisible circle inside of reasons and seasons. The stitches of the earth connect us to our feet which may buckle our knees and hear us pray, *"why am I buried inside this darkest cave?"*

And the sun's wind will answer,

"You are with the roots of your ancestors. Just listen. Rest. Go very slow. Watch how your footsteps are held by the earth. And when ready you'll release as a seedling knows darkness has shades of supple grey letting light into the questions that already have answers blooming inside of your heart and soul."

Loneliness Has a Companion

*A*long the horizon a layer of clouds eased into the shape of love; mineral like in her colors, sourced from the kindness of the earth and yet gentle as handmade parchment.

This love wears all the bits and pieces of imperfections; qualities that show vulnerability, value, and hears voices on the breeze of midnight's solitudes.

There's a longing to share the simple joys of telling dreams, showing care, and receiving it too. It's a need to be part of sentimental sensing smiles, coveted by tender tones of—I love you—no matter what the mood.

The acorn's oak of love is reflected by the moon on the stillest and deepest waters unfolding a blossoming circumference that understands; loneliness has a companion with an unyielding cosmos, only wishing it would hold her hand.

A Compass of Compassion

Quiet with me
a river of spirits
so that the raging flow
can find a pinhole
to navigate the rocky edges
somehow lost
as if a compass
has turned the waters
cave cold.

Breathe with her underwater
as magic can stitch gills
in the colors of
blacks and blues
only to find a fairy
all alone.

The doorway is without a door
but the sprite doesn't know;
her soul sister
hands her a compass
of compassion
and welcomes her
to a new and safe home.

Gathered in the richness
of silence and time,
are quilts of gentle courage;
patchworked of faded cotton dresses.

Those calicos reminiscent
of tiny floral meadows
dreaming of skinned knees
now kissed.

Riverbeds now dry;
seeking a safe hand
now held. When time
forgets time
and becomes now.

Sweet Breeze

Quiet days
can have a feel
and color
of an unseen sunset.

It's a reverie of waves
enveloping a native coastline
where souls speak
the gift of tides.

It's a love note
written by a warm
sweet breeze.

And a freedom
to dream
into the shelter
of her lush lulls of still
as Nature
rolls over cloud
and dim hill
hearing flowers summon
a hummingbird's sigh.

Shadows Are Our Best Teachers

*O*ftentimes we can't see the how or why of life's trajectory guiding us in this convoluted world. Sometimes it is the quieter souls that gift us room to shine and the more confident ones who understand our shyness needs support as we find the words and actions to complement our growth.

Likewise, we can offer our skillsets to amplify the shadows others may hide behind—not knowing their worth.

In this process there's an inner voice; the voice of our intuition that we start to notice.

We begin to lean into that wisdom and follow her lead.

Of course, there are days we still get triggered and trip over our toes, however we try again because we trust a little more in ourselves. Not only believing those pillar-like tree friends who line our path and walk beside us, but we have more self-confidence.

The past seems like an arrow pointing us forward and still knowing we need to meander down quiet roads to rest, regroup, recount what brings us the biggest joys; such as the need to craft a rowboat in a set of clouds and drift and drift.

We also learn to smile easier, a silent thank you when someone notices and shares how much we do.

We start to feel the compliments connecting with our body and our soul weeps through and fills the cracks unseen; this compound is honey-like and soothing, warm, and safe.

We see our needs breaching the ocean's horizon as if breathing for the first time.

Our quirks are accepted, and we no longer feel as lost. The trembling seasons of generations have pressed through into new growth and her roots and branches reveal our full colors are divine.

Moonlight

Last night
when moonlight
was half-lit
I sat half-dark.

Unbeknownst to its magic
a ring of opal-like stars
selflessly hummed
a perfect pitch that sensed
an inner pained collectiveness.

It carved into me
the need to be seen
and to begin a round sound of
tonal margins so fiery blue
hearts began unfolding from
generational vilified hues.

Witnessed is the feminine form
unashamed and transparent;
soft is kind
intelligent is strong
sensitivity is a gift
and equal is the norm.

The stars repeated their hum
as a circle of 5ths
in every major and minor key
amplifying the harmonies
until I could no longer sit
but dance
in the freest forest-like form.

The control that
had me suppressed

by man's oppression
was left on the ground;
starkly seen by a half-lit moon;
where the half-dark side of me
saw the truth.

Sea Glass

My dreams were made of sea glass.
Vintage in their knowing,
a whale's dove-blue
diving deeper
to bestow sight
next to pure and her shadows,
infinite in their complexities
of living on a spinning orb
governed by the moon;
following ageless stitches
of patchwork quilts
as they labored
an unfair harvest.
Black cotton's history
in fields where sundown
didn't come soon. A dry
burnt taste of earth ceased
the acrimonious oxygen
only to be held with respect
in the dreams of sea glass
and a whale's dove blue.

Dream Child

Wild me a vision
that begins with
small
big
shy
loud
soft
steps
to welcome
the dream child
who came into this world with,
purest
fullest
truest
deepest
sincerest
qualities of sensitive;
unceasingly airy grace
voiced through subtle
coaxed by mirrored metaphors
that draw us and repel us to
this dance
this life
this accord.
May this vision
be our wildest song
to begin us
once more.

When Dreams Must Die

Some dreams must die. Those dreams that hold us back. The ones that carry us far under into what 'should be' and 'could be' and 'wish we were'. But there's a tinge of real and it keeps growing.

Now it is a full throat grasp that cuts deeper into a very knowing place. It catches us at every page turn and throws us into a heart-spin. Our throats howl like an animal betrayed.

Repeating 'you know what you must do. Die to a way that was because it isn't the current path for you.'

Singing the Blues tastes lonely but it's better to honor the layers of grief.

We know without a doubt what our soul is telling us. It's time to let that dream die a soft fatal crunch where the wind blows still, and where the lands lay frozen.

At some point, a new tomorrow will begin to feather a brilliant wild—a fresh way, a clear way.

But first, some dreams must die before we can begin anew.

Braid My Thoughts

I'll close my eyes now
and braid my thoughts
over the back of worn blue chair
letting the genesis of dreams
marinate with silence
and unfold when
ready to be shared.

This Much I Know

We are the dream.
Listen. Walk. Be strong. Be real. Be gentle.
Crumble like sand. Become a beach.
Follow the stars.
Weep loud. Weep soft. Close your eyes hard.
Rest.
Be your heart. Honor your power. Speak directly.
Silence inner criticism.
Stand together. Hold tight. Let go.
Support each other.
Discover your thunder.
Be a river.
Build to unite.
Be the holy sound of you.

About the Author

CAROLYN RIKER, MA, LMHC is a poet and a writer influenced by nature, music, and daydreaming. Creativity, imagination, and sensitivity are her superpowers. She is also a mom of two incredible young adults and shares countless hours of conversation with her plump ginger kitty. In addition to writing, Carolyn is a Licensed Mental Health Counselor who specializes in working with Highly Sensitive People. Her private practice gives her flexibility to write. You can learn more about her by visiting her website at:

www.carolynriker.com.